TOM JACKSON'S

INTERVIEW
EXPRESS

D1374173

Also by Tom Jackson

TOM JACKSON'S
INTERVIEW EXPRESS

Tom Jackson and Bill Buckingham

TIMES BOOKS

RANDOM HOUSE

To all job seekers who are prepared to negotiate a future
that taps into their greatest potential.

Library of Congress Cataloging-in-Publication Data

Jackson, Tom.
    Tom Jackson's interview express / by Tom Jackson & Bill
Buckingham.
        p. cm.
    ISBN 0-8129-2129-1
    1. Employment interviewing   2. Job hunting. I. Buckingham, Bill.
II. Title.
HF5549.5.I6J32   1993
650.14—dc20   92-56822

Manufactured in the United States of America

9   8   7   6   5   4   3   2

First Edition

Design and production by ROBERT BULL DESIGN

CONTENTS

5. MAKING A POWERFUL IMPRESSION

6. PAINTING A PICTURE OF SUCCESS

7. PROVING YOUR POINT

8. CLOSING IN ON THE OFFER

9. GOING FOR THE GOLD

10. FINAL PREPARATION

INTERVIEW EXPRESS PLANNER

TOM JACKSON'S

INTERVIEW EXPRESS

INTERVIEWING FOR BREAKTHROUGHS

The interview is the central event in every job search.

The way you conduct your next interview can make you or break you. Effective interviewing will lead to good job offers; poor interviewing will keep you stuck.

This book gives you an important advantage in your interviews. It is an easy-to-use digest of proven strategies and tactics that will sharpen your preparation, increase your confidence, and amplify positive self-expression.

Use these ideas and suggestions to negotiate a future that taps into your greatest potential.

The Interview Express Planner

Preparation is key. On pages 69–85 you will find the Interview Express Planner, a series of questions and forms to organize your thinking in advance of each interview. Make copies of this planner and use it as a preparation guide before each interview.

Throughout the book you will see an icon like this, directing you to a section in the planner.

☞ Turn to the Interview Express Planner, Section A on page 71.

To apply what you are reading to your specific needs, go to that section and answer the questions.

An alternative is to work through the planner from beginning to end after you finish reading the book.

Either way, the payoff is enormous in preparing you for the interview.

Critical Success Factors

Here are seven key principles for conducting job-winning interviews. Each is explained in greater depth in subsequent chapters.

1. Have a clear picture in mind of the job you want to do and why, from the employer's point of view, you should be given the opportunity to do it.
2. Know what the employer really needs and how you can fill the requirements.
3. Demonstrate your competence by thoroughly preparing for the interview. Anticipate questions and rehearse the key points you want to make.
4. Speak in a way that helps the employer picture you in the job.
5. In your dress, bearing, and speech present yourself in a way that builds the employer's confidence in your capability and enthusiasm.
6. Elicit ongoing feedback from the interviewer and make appropriate adjustments to your presentation.
7. Negotiate salary and benefits intelligently and assertively. Know how to communicate and get paid your full worth.

A Vision of Success

Vision (a mental picture of what is possible) ignites motivation. Painting a picture of your future success in the mind of the interviewer can communicate far more than just a recitation of past duties and accomplishments.

You can accomplish this by giving examples and asking the right questions. Use words to create images: "How do you *see* this in operation?" or "What do you think that would *look* like?" or "Can you *picture* . . ."

PERSONAL VISION EXERCISE

Take a moment to picture yourself in a productive and satisfying future job. Start by quieting your mind, eliminating distractions or interruptions. Take a deep breath and . . .

- Imagine walking into your new workspace. Examine the colors and shapes, the furniture and fixtures that fill it. See the view out your window.

- You are working successfully. What are you doing? What tools are you using? How are you using your body and mind? Whom do you work with and for? How do you communicate with these people? See the value you create and the impact you make.

- Take a few moments to complete your visualization, and then make notes of what you saw. This will help you clearly see yourself as a success in your new job.

☞ To make notes on your visualization of future success, turn to the Interview Express Planner, Section A on page 71.

Winning and Winning

Employers *want* to hire. Most companies are committed to bringing together the best people possible, so the purpose of the interview is to *select,* not to reject.

Interviewers register tangible and intangible factors in making their decisions about whom to hire. The tangible factors (how you dress, your education, your past accomplishments, for example) are easily evaluated, but intangible factors like confidence, responsiveness, energy, and enthusiasm are also equally important.

EMPLOYER INSIGHT
"It's relatively simple to choose between two people who have similar credentials. I want to hire the one who is excited about working for us and is willing to jump right in and get the job done."

Add the following to your vision of yourself as a success:

- A positive, alert, and enthusiastic attitude.
- Effective, direct communication; able to make a point and ask a pointed question.
- Willingness to do more than is required.
- A winner's presentation in dress and self-confidence.
- Versatility—the ability to change direction easily and without complaint.
- A commitment to winning.

Controlling the Interview

To succeed in interviews, you must subtly manage the direction, rather than just follow the lead of the interviewer.

CONTROL STRATEGIES

- Know in advance what the company is seeking.
- Prepare an agenda for the interview, listing the points you want to make.
- Help the interviewer visualize your success in the job.
- Stay attuned to word usage, innuendo, and body language, your own as well as your interviewer's.
- Be aware of how much time has been allocated.
- Refer to your notes during the interview.
- Elicit ongoing feedback.
- Ask questions that will steer the interview back to subjects that reveal your strong points, or to get the information you need to appraise the firm.

Assert Your Value

Break out of your (smaller) image of yourself. Go into the interview willing to assert what you can accomplish when you operate at full throttle. Step beyond old assumptions, opinions, and beliefs about yourself. Become the solution to a problem. Believe they need you more than you need them.

Communicate for Action

Successful interviewing rests on your ability to convey to the interviewer your personal vision of on-the-job success. You should reinforce this idea with a clear statement of the value you offer, with precise questions, and with requests to proceed to the next step in the hiring process.

POWER TOOLS FOR COMMUNICATION

• Know what results you want to produce.

• Eliminate negativity, gossip, complaining, and indirection from your comments. If you've got nothing positive to contribute, just listen.

• Avoid being tentative. Eliminate words and phrases such as *possibly, somewhat, I hope, I'll do my best, I'll try, more or less.*

• Refer to your accomplishments, not just your responsibilities. Include specifics where possible. Use active verbs to describe your accomplishments: "I *designed . . . directed, researched, trimmed,"* etc.

• Be positive, talking more of opportunities than problems.

• Make suggestions that direct the employer's thinking into new channels: *"What would it look like if you combined those two functions?"* or *"How far do you think we could go if several departments collaborated on this project?"*

2

OPENING DOORS

All your research, resume writing, and networking are useless unless you set up an interview.

To get an interview, you need three things:

1. Clarity about the kind of job or jobs you want.

2. A list of companies that interest you and the people within those companies whom you want to meet.

3. Something valuable to say to arouse an employer's interest in seeing you.

Building Network Contacts

Once you know the companies that interest you, you'll need contacts. The best way to get an interview is to find someone who has influence in the organization to recommend you. Even if you don't know anyone to call directly, you may know someone who knows someone who can reach a decision maker in the company.

Make a list of people you know and people you'd like to know. Get these contacts to open doors to other people in the organizations you want to reach.

- If you know someone who works for the company, ask him to find out to whom you should speak. See if he can set up a meeting for you.

- Ask a trade or professional association in your field for potential contacts. If you don't belong to a trade association, apply for provisional membership, attend meetings, or join as a full member. Your network will expand enormously.

- Attend trade shows and business-sponsored events. Strangers can become fast friends.

- Contact the editors of trade journals or writers who cover your field and ask them for referrals.

- Contact the local chamber of commerce, business clubs, and associations. Attend their meetings.

- If you're a college graduate, contact your alumni association and members of your graduating class or fraternity. Check yearbooks and directories.

- Look up a college professor in your field or a former boss or colleague.

- Speak with a management consultant or placement counselor in your field.

- Contact a banker or lawyer with a professional connection to the company.

- Confer with a customer or client of your targeted employer.

Keep accurate and up-to-date records of these network contacts. Include each name, organization, title, phone number, how you were introduced, etc.

☞ To record your network contacts, turn to the Interview Express Planner, Section B on page 72.

Gatekeepers

Most organizations have a tight system to make sure that people coming for interviews "belong there." Secretaries, personnel staff, and voice mail all work to screen out unknown visitors and callers.

TIPS FOR GETTING AROUND THE SECRETARY

- Know the name of the person you want to reach and ask directly and informally for that person: *"Is he in?"* instead of *"May I please speak to Mrs. Perry?"*

- In order to keep the initiative in your hands, leave as few messages as possible. Avoid repeated messages. If the person isn't in, simply ask, *"When do you expect her?"* then *"Thank you. I'll call her back."* If asked, *"Would you like to leave your name and number?"* you might say, *"I'm going to be away from my phone for a while. I'll call back."*

- Avoid being defensive about the purpose of the call. Never say you are looking for a job. Identify yourself and speak as someone already working in the field in question. For example: If asked what your call is about, *"Jane Altschuler suggested I call about a movie script that is being considered."* If the secretary says, *"May I help you with that?"* you can respond, *"I need to discuss this matter with her personally. When do you expect her? I'll call back."*

- If the secretary wants to pass you on to the personnel department, don't resist, but continue to pursue a meeting with your initial contact. Try this: *"Yes, I do plan to meet with the personnel department; however, there are some important questions I'd like to ask Mr. Grijns before I approach them. When do you expect him?"*

- When you call the company's switchboard, get the direct number of the person you want to speak with so you can reach him or her early or late in the working day. This is the best time to avoid the gatekeepers.

DEALING WITH VOICE MAIL

Here are some suggestions in dealing with voice-mail systems:

- In general, avoid leaving messages. Keep trying until you reach the person.

- Prior to calling for an interview, work out your clear, concise, self-promoting opening statement and write out your key points. Have a shorter message ready to leave on voice mail if necessary, such as: *"Mr. Black, Jane Farley suggested I call you to talk about your new project. I'd appreciate a return call. You can reach me for the next day or two at the following number. . ."*

Safety in numbers: It's a big psychological boost to have a number of people to call at any one time. Keep all names and phone numbers well organized on a computer or 3" x 5" index cards. Start calling when you have a list of twenty-five to thirty people. At least some of them will respond favorably. A little success will encourage you to continue.

Influencers:
Greasing the Skids for Your Interviews

Influencers are people who can make introductions, pull strings, say good things about you, and provide valuable feedback. You can also gain influence through articles you have written, published reports, and other data you can provide before, during, or after your interview.

If you have a friend who knows someone in the organization who could be an influencer, try to meet with that person so he or she can get to know you firsthand.

Thank the people who have been helpful and keep them informed.

The Decision Maker

You may have several interviews with someone you think has the power to make the final decision only to find out her boss has the final word.

As you engage in the interview process, find out how and by whom the final decision will be made. Usually a senior level person makes a recommendation that is then approved by a department head. Your personnel contact can give you accurate information about how this process will work.

The steps of even the best job search proceed something like this:

No, No, No, No, No, No, No, No, No, No, *YES!*

Don't let a "no" distract you or slow you down; it's one step closer to *yes.*

Phone Meeting Versus Real Meeting

The purpose of the telephone interview is to create sufficient interest for a face-to-face interview. Try not to let the telephone contact replace the face-to-face interview.

When you call someone to request a meeting, have a statement ready about the value you can produce. Also, you should have a specific reason for requesting the meeting, such as: *"I've been doing some research about the XYZ account and have some ideas I'd like to share with you. Could we meet toward the middle of this coming week?"* See Chapter 4 for more details on telephone interviews.

Making Your Point on a Cold Call

Here are seven ways to give your cold call maximum impact:

1. Organize. Prepare notes and rehearse your phone presentation in advance.

2. Request a meeting rather than an interview. Have your calendar at hand and suggest one or two possible dates.

3. Describe your intention as wanting to discuss ways you can contribute value to the organization rather than looking for a job. The latter makes you sound needy, whereas the discussion of real possibilities suggests mutual benefit.

4. Get to the point quickly: *"I'm calling to see if we can set up a short meeting next week while I'm in your area."* Or *"I'd like to show you some examples of my work and find out more about what's happening with your new products."*

5. Expect resistance. People aren't inherently interested in setting up meetings with strangers.

6. Listen to the employer's resistance and objections and acknowledge them.

7. Continue to press for a meeting in a way that suggests it could be valuable to the employer. For example: *"I know you are a pro in this field, and so am I. It might be useful to both of us to discuss where the business is going. Would you be willing to meet for a half hour?"*

☞ To plan your telephone message, turn to the Interview Express Planner, Section C on page 73.

EMPLOYER INSIGHT
"Many people call to ask if I have any job openings. When I say no (which is usually the case) they thank me and sign off. Even if there are no openings I am generally willing to meet people who sound like they have true potential. I never know what talent I will need in the future."

Information Interview
versus the Job Interview

People in the field will often grant a twenty-minute information-only interview to someone who expresses sincere interest in the field. Information interviews can be conducted by telephone, although they are better in person.

Don't use an information interview to get your foot in the door for a real job interview. Employers would consider this exploitative. It is acceptable to contact the employer again after several weeks to remind her of the previous meeting, and ask if she is willing to discuss real job possibilities.

Prepare a list of questions to ask in your information interviews. Take notes and ask for the names of other people you can contact. Thank the people who give you the information and add them to your network contacts.

Creating Possibility

Your quest to work for a company need not be based on a particular job opening. In the rapidly changing work world, a job can be created if you present yourself as a possible solution to current or future problems that have yet to be translated into job openings. In your message, talk about trends, strategies, and new directions in your meetings rather than job slots that need filling.

3

BE PREPARED

To your prospective employers, one of the clearest indications of your ability to manage a job is how prepared you are for the interview. Not being prepared wastes one of your major employment opportunities.

Spend a couple of hours getting ready for each interview.

Seven Things to Know in Advance

Review the following list several days before an interview to give yourself time to prepare.

1. **Who are they (the prospective employers) and what do they do?** Who owns the company? What are its products and services? How does the department or group for which you're interviewing relate to the whole company?

2. **What has the company done?** Know some history. Has it recently merged or been deregulated? What have its last two or three years been like? Know about the industry of which it's part. What is the company's growth rate? Who are its competitors?

3. **Where are they headed?** Know current predictions for the company and industry. What new products are on the horizon? How does the company stand in national and international competition? If they have new leadership, what goals have they announced?

4. **What is the competition?** Where is this company at an advantage or disadvantage? What are the trends in technology and profits? Get the names of the company's biggest competitors and know what advantages or disadvantages those competitors have.

5. **What are the success factors?** What influences the company's ability to achieve its targets? One set of factors is external and

includes the economy, competition, and technology. Other factors are more internal, such as cost cutting, revitalization, and penetration of new markets.

6. **How can the job you are pursuing contribute to the company's success?** This may take more interpretation than research, but you want to have a clear idea of how the department and job relate to the future success of the organization. Even if the job you want is at a lower level, you need to know how it relates to the whole.

7. **Three successes.** Be prepared to describe three specific things you have done that demonstrate how you can contribute to the organization's future success.

If you are interviewing with a smaller, privately owned firm, it will be harder to find information on its history and strategies, but it is essential to do so. Find out about comparable businesses that are better known and assume that people in similar situations will face similar challenges. Check product brochures and magazines.

EMPLOYER INSIGHT

"Four out of five applicants don't know much beyond the obvious about our company. It turns me off to have to do their homework for them. When an applicant really knows what we are doing and what's going on in the industry, she has a great advantage."

Insider Information

We are referring here not to secret or proprietary information, but to facts that are available to the public if requested. Insider information is not easy to obtain, but very valuable. You have to make a special effort to pay particular attention to company publications, news releases, etc.

Information to look for:

1. **The company's mission statement:** Find out if it has published one and get a copy of it.

2. **Strategic objectives:** Check stock writeups, annual reports, or internal documents.

3. **Corporate values**: Often published and available to employees and customers in brochures.

4. **Current problems, challenges, and changes**: If a public company, this will be in stock analyst reports. Try trade journals and business publications.

5. **Organizational changes**: Is the company moving toward centralization? decentralization? Has it embarked on any major changes—for example, from a domestic to a global orientation, or from product orientation to customer orientation?

Hot Sources

- Anyone you know employed by the company
- Corporate public relations; personnel handouts
- Trade journals, investment experts, Standard & Poor's
- Company newsletters and product announcements
- Industry specialists
- Competitors and suppliers
- The business reference section of any major public or university library.

Preparing for the Interview

Prepare the following before each interview:

- **An agenda**

  List the main points you want to communicate about yourself, and five or six questions you want to ask based on your research. Make notes to take with you to the interview and consult them.

- **A good defense**

  Anticipate questions the employer might ask you (see Chapter 6) and anticipate any objections that could stand in the way of a job offer. Prepare and practice responses to these questions and objections.

- **Practice**

  Role plays will polish your presentation and make you more comfortable. Practice interviews point up areas where you need improvement. See Chapter 7 for a list of questions you can use in mock interviews.

- **What to bring with you**

    Take notes, pad and pen, relevant news articles, and extra copies of your resume. Have exact directions to the interview site and parking area (if necessary) and get there with time to spare.

The Creative Advantage

To be competitive with other candidates you must exceed expectations. Consider how you can expand the employer's thinking about the job. Train yourself to think beyond nuts and bolts to the future of the organization by asking questions like these:

- How can you offer far more value than is required by the job description?
- What are some innovations in technology, training, etc., that the employer should consider for the job in the future?
- How can you make the employer's job easier?
- How can you motivate and inspire others in their work?
- How can the job more actively serve the company's customers, internal or external?

☞ To organize your pre-interview research, turn to the Interview Express Planner, Section D on page 74.

4

A GALLERY OF INTERVIEWS

Impromptu Interview

Impromptu conversations can be sources of information and further contacts. As you meet people socially, ask what they do at their jobs. Describe your work interests in a general way. If you are not working, avoid complaining about it.

If you are interested in what someone tells you about his work or company, look for an opportunity to arrange a more in-depth meeting. Get a business card. Express your interest by asking, *"How is your company doing?"* or *"How long have you been at the firm?"* or *"What kind of work does your department do?"*

Participate in volunteer or church groups and professional associations. Once you have established a relationship you can build further contacts.

The Headhunter Interview

Headhunters help employers fill jobs. There are two main types:

- **Executive search firms**: consultants retained by a specific employer to recruit candidates according to that employer's specifications.

- **Employment agencies**: firms that fill a variety of jobs and look for applicants across a range. The agency is usually paid a percentage fee by the hiring employer.

EXECUTIVE SEARCH FIRMS

If someone from an executive search firm initiates an interview with you, it is either to have you suggest the names of other potential candidates or because she already knows something about you and wants to know more.

If you are seriously being considered as a candidate, explore the situation even if you are not ready to move. Ask the interviewer to describe the position and organization. If the call comes unexpectedly, reschedule it so you can prepare your questions.

Even if you are interested, play hard to get. Don't commit to any salary levels over the phone. Learn more about the company and the position first.

Executive recruiters are well informed about the fields for which they are recruiting. You can ask them about current trends in the industry and what qualities and expertise a particular company finds desirable.

Executive recruiters need to maintain contacts, so you may be able to initiate an interview with one. This is best done through a referral from a client or a potential employer. Use the *Directory of Executive Recruiters* (Kennedy Publications) at your local library to locate search firms in your profession. If you are given a courtesy interview, use it to gather information rather than to pinpoint a particular job.

- Find out current, local, national, and international industry trends.
- Ask for a critique of your resume.
- Find out about salary and benefits packages in your field.
- Ask for the names of other search firms active in your field.

EMPLOYMENT AGENCIES

Contact employment agencies: nothing ventured, nothing gained. Clarify fee arrangements at the outset.

- Try to have someone the agency does business with refer you to a specific counselor with whom you can establish rapport.
- Before meeting with the agency counselor, be clear about your job direction. Find out what field he specializes in, and if it's not yours, ask him to recommend you to someone in the agency who does work in your field.
- Prepare a written description of your job target and requirements, including location, size of company, and position, to give to the counselor. The more precise you are about what you want, the better the counselor will be able to help you.

- Treat the counselor with the same respect you would an employer representative.

- Find out up front what the employment consultant can do and what she expects you to do.

- If a particular company interests you, ask the counselor if the agency has a contact there. Know, however, that if the agency recommends you to that employer and you land a job, the agency is probably entitled to a placement fee. If you made contacts earlier, let the counselor know about them to avoid future conflict.

- Explore salary ranges, but don't expect the final word from the counselor. It's in the agent's interest to get you placed quickly, regardless of the salary offered.

- Agency interviews are generally shorter than hiring interviews. At the end of your agency interview, ask what the plan of action is, how you can facilitate it, and when to follow up. Take notes.

Out-of-Town, Employer-Paid Interviews

Employers hiring upper-level managers and skilled workers frequently pay to bring in out-of-towners for an interview. Before agreeing to an interview with an out-of-town employer, learn precisely how you will be reimbursed for expenses, the length of your stay, whom you'll be expected to meet, and the schedule for the visit. Ask for a written itinerary.

Usually a host interviewer (generally from personnel) will be your guide through several interviews. Establish a solid relationship with this person, and ask for his or her feedback along the way. Adjust your presentation accordingly.

SENIOR OFFICIAL FLYBY

At some point, you're likely to be introduced to a senior official. This is usually not an in-depth interview (unless you'll be working directly with that person), but it is an important formality.

This is a good time to demonstrate your knowledge of the company. For example: *"I was impressed with the claims department's move to multi-tasking to improve client service,"* or *"I was interested to see that when you reorganized, several department operations were integrated."*

Have one or two senior-level power questions to ask such as: *"During the day we've had some conversations about the need to shift from domestic to global strategies. From your own point of view, how quickly could this happen?"*

The visit might conclude with a debriefing session with your host. Ask what steps will follow and how you can facilitate the decision-making process. If you think you missed something along the way, explain this to your host so he or she can pass it along. On your way home, plan your follow-up strategy.

The Screening Interview

As powerful as the telephone is, it's frustrating as an interview medium. Lack of visual contact inhibits your ability to control the conversation.

The purpose of the screening interview by phone or in person is to eliminate unqualified candidates in less than thirty minutes. Many screening interviews are conducted according to a checklist, and the interviewer might not be particularly responsive to your taking the initiative. Do it gently.

Test your screener's familiarity with the company, the position, and you. Does she have your resume in front of her? Has she read it? Avoid embarrassing the screener if you sense a lack of knowledge about the field; you'll want to keep her in your corner.

One alternative is to try to convert the screening call into a personal meeting. If that's not possible, find out who is calling and set a convenient time to return the call. If the caller insists on continuing the conversation right then, ask her to hold while you get pad and pen, and use this pause to gain your composure and remind yourself to screen the company before it screens you. Some tips:

- Find out what the caller knows about you. Has she read your resume? Is she a decision maker? What is the purpose of the call?

- In anticipation of such a call, have a list ready of a few questions to ask and points to make about yourself.

- Listen carefully to questions posed and, if necessary, ask for clarification before answering.

- Speak slowly and specifically, and ask for confirmation: *"Does that answer your question?"* or *"Would you like more information about that?"*

- If a tough question comes up, ask the screener to qualify it so you can focus your answer.

- Be pleasant. Your screener may be a new employee needing encouragement or an old hand needing a breath of fresh air. Most will reciprocate your goodwill.

- Ask for a review at the end of the interview. *"You helped me cover a lot of ground. On the basis of this information, will you recommend me for further consideration?"*

- If you didn't do well in the screening interview, you might attempt a strategy to secure another interview anyway: *"I have some ideas about the job that differ from the way it's been described. Could you arrange a meeting with the hiring manager so I could discuss my ideas with him?"*

- Close with a request for a personal meeting.

The Campus Interview

Most colleges have a period during which corporations visit the campus to recruit the best of the current crop of graduates. Both multinational firms and regional firms participate. Campus interviews are often set up by the various college departments: business, engineering, nursing, etc.

CAMPUS INTERVIEW TIPS

- Competition is tough. Many students take themselves out of contention by not knowing enough about the company. Do lots of research and role-play in preparation.

- Participate in campus placement-office activities before the interviewing begins.

- Since the interview may be only fifteen minutes long, make your presentation short and powerful.

- Ask students who have already been interviewed to give you a sense of the interviewer's style so you can respond to it.

- If your grades are low, be prepared to explain why and how they do not reflect your future potential.

- Extracurricular activities count. If working to cover expenses prevented you from participating in such activities, describe with pride the responsibility you've assumed.
- Don't limit yourself to jobs within your field of study. Be willing to engage a recruiter in a discussion of your possible contributions to other areas of the company.
- Dress as a professional, not as a student (which can eliminate you automatically).
- Reserve salary discussions for a later meeting.
- Ask for contacts in certain areas of the company the recruiter might not be familiar with so you can follow up on your own if necessary.
- Take care of the interviewer. Ask if you can get her a cup of coffee or be of any assistance during the day.
- Be willing to ask tough questions, even of a pleasant interviewer.
- Demonstrate confidence in yourself and your potential value to the company.
- Speak positively about your school and professors. Do not gossip or complain. The interviewer could be an alumnus or a friend of the person you're maligning.
- In closing, request your interviewer's business card, and make arrangements for a follow-up meeting.

CAMPUS RECRUITER INSIGHT

"During a day, I might meet twenty people. Nineteen of them are just students—they look and act like students. One, however, is a future professional. He's a sharp dresser, has done his research about our business, and knows what he's going for."

Managing the Team Interview

In certain situations, especially where professional and academic positions are at stake, you may find yourself at a team interview with several people from the organization. The team interview is expedient for the company and stressful for the candidate.

Here are some ways to prepare:

- Before your interview learn the names and titles of those on the panel and write them on a 3" x 5" index card to bring to the interview. Ask about the relationship of each of these people to the job for which you are applying.

- Make a strong introduction by taking a moment to establish eye contact and firmly shake hands with each person.

- Use names freely (first or surnames, as appropriate). This gives you an element of control.

- Ask specific questions of each interviewer while making eye contact and addressing each one by name. This gives you an element of control.

- If you are interviewing with a complete working unit, ask how it functions and to what degree the members work together and independently.

- Bring a copy of your resume for each interviewer.

Second and Third Interviews

If you have been invited back for a second or third interview, congratulate yourself. So far you have been successful. However, you're now on a short list of fierce competitors.

Once you've passed the personnel department's screening process, you'll begin to meet people you could be working with. Your second interview will probably be more detailed and technical than the first.

You now need to pay *more* attention to spotlighting your value. Be prepared to answer tough and stressful questions. Some tips:

- Contact your original interviewer to thank him for recommending you and to ask how you should prepare for the next round.

- Learn the name, title, and role of the next interviewer in advance. After this interview, will there be another farther up the chain of command?

- Review your notes from the first interview. What questions were emphasized? What did you find out about the firm? Conduct whatever further research is necessary. You now know someone in the firm (the first interviewer) who can provide a well of information, but don't take advantage of this relationship.

- If the second interview is with the same person as the first, refer to earlier topics and develop them further. Demonstrate your ability to pay attention and retain information.

- As you approach the end of the second interview, ask about the salary range for the job. You gain an advantage by raising the subject. (See Chapter 9 for more detailed salary hints.)

- Listen attentively. Often a question telegraphs a decision, for example: *"We think you'd do quite well in this job. Are there any limitations on the amount of travel you will be willing to do?"* or *"If we make you an offer, when would you be able to start?"*

- Don't be too eager with your answers. If given an offer, reserve the right to take a few days to consider it.

Interviews over Meals

Try to avoid having your first interview at breakfast, lunch, or dinner. The preoccupation with eating and informal discussion that naturally accompany meals combine to dilute the impact you want to make.

However, a lunch or dinner meeting at a second or third interview is usually a good sign, since most basic information has already been exchanged. This will be a more social get-together.

SOME DOS AND DON'TS

- Order simple dishes that you can eat neatly. Avoid expensive items.

- Decline alcoholic beverages.

- Don't criticize food, location, or service. It might be your interviewer's favorite.

- Eat while your host is speaking, so you'll be ready to speak when it is your turn.

5

MAKING A POWERFUL IMPRESSION

Employers don't always hire the person with the best qualifications. As much as you would like to believe in an impartial process, the most qualified person does not necessarily get the job offer. It's usually the person who makes the best impression.

Think About This

An "impression" is the total impact a person makes by his or her posture, manner of dress, way of speaking, confidence, and other intangible factors. It does not rely on any one element, but is the effect of all factors working together to communicate power.

Pay attention to the impression you make and people will pay attention to you.

EMPLOYER INSIGHT

"It's tough to anticipate how an applicant will work out if hired. Experience and degrees don't tell the full story. In the end, I usually rely on how the person presents herself or himself in the interview. It's in the way they dress, the questions they ask, their willingness to challenge what I say and present new ideas, and their interest in making a contribution."

Sweaty Palms

It is tough to put yourself on the line for an interview. An inner voice chips away at your self-confidence. You feel like a person wrongly accused of a crime approaching a hostile judge. Butterflies in your stomach, a high-pitched, squeaky voice stuck in your throat, hands that don't know what to do, heart palpitations, sweaty palms, wobbly legs: All these are symptoms of the fear of rejection.

Ten Ways to Restore Calm

1. **Dress so that you feel successful.**
   The right clothing and accessories are an investment that pays off handsomely in increased positive responses from employers. (See page 34 for more details.)

2. **Know more about the employer than the employer knows about you.**
   Knowledge is an antidote to anxiety. Lessen your fear of the unknown by being thoroughly prepared (see Chapter 3).

3. **Simplify the process.**
   There are only five things you need to accomplish in the first interview:
   - Find out what the employer needs.
   - Communicate clearly what you can contribute.
   - Be prepared to answer questions about your experience and education.
   - Get feedback and meet possible objections.
   - Push toward the next stage of negotiations.

4. **Remember, employers want to hire.**
   Remind yourself that employers need qualified people, and you are one of them.

5. **Create a mental picture of yourself operating at peak performance.**
   Before to every interview, take time to imagine yourself making a great impression.

6. **Practice with friends.**
   Find people to role-play the interview with you and give you feedback. Practice answering the tough questions (see Chapter 10).

7. **Make notes to help yourself.**
   List the main points you want to make and the questions you want to ask on 3" x 5" index cards to consult during the interview.

8. **You're nervous. Admit it.**
   A little stage fright is expected at an interview. It is more difficult to pretend you're not scared than to admit that you are.

9. Give yourself enough room and time.

Prepare the day before and make a short list of points to review just prior to the interview. Get a good night's sleep. Get to the interview location early and walk around the block to reduce stress. Arrive at the reception area ten minutes prior to your interview. Use the time to visualize again the powerful impression you will make.

10. Breathe.

You are most effective with a relaxed mind and body. Take a moment to think between questions and answers, breathe slowly, and speak precisely.

The Power Start

The adage "You never get a second chance to make a first impression" is true. How you look, how you sound, how you respond will frame your relationship with the interviewer.

Every meeting starts with a greeting. When your interviewer arrives in the reception area, rise (leave your belongings where they are), take two or three steps forward, look directly at your interviewer, extend your hand, smile, say hello, and introduce yourself. Remember the interviewer's name.

When invited, get your things and follow briskly to the interview room. If a secretary or clerical person meets you in the lobby, accord them the same respect you would the interviewer.

Positioning

On entering the office, look for a convenient place to hang your coat and put your briefcase. Wait for the interviewer to indicate where you should sit.

Keep your body posture relaxed but not slouched. Do not smoke, even if you are invited to do so. Three to five minutes of small talk is expected. If there is something in the office that is interesting or special (a piece of artwork, a great view, an unusual library), comment on it.

Get the interviewer to speak first by asking an open question: *"How is the business doing?"* or *"What attracted you to this company?"* Listen to what he or she says.

"Can I Get You Something to Drink?"

The interviewer may offer you a soda or coffee. If you are too nervous to balance a steaming cup of coffee, ask for water or juice. If the offer seems only pro forma say, *"Thank you, but not now."* Don't ask for refreshments if they're not offered, even if your interviewer has some. If the beverage offer is made when you are well into the interview, take this as a sign that things are going well and accept.

Building Rapport

Rapport is a feeling of mutual trust between you and the interviewer that allows for openness and a free flow of information. Once rapport is established, the interview will become a more interactive conversation about possibilities rather than a simple series of questions and answers.

How to build rapport:

- **See the interviewer as a person,** not a function. Speak to her as you would to a colleague.

- **Address the interviewer formally** and, if invited, by her first name. Use the name of the department or company in conversation as often as you can.

- **Ask how much time has been allotted for the interview.** Remind the interviewer when there are five or ten minutes left and ask for more time if you need it.

- **Speak the interviewer's language.** Personnel interviewers may not know all of the jargon of the position. Use lay terms if the interviewer is not familiar with technical terms.

- **Demonstrate that you are listening.** Physical gestures (nodding, facial expressions, etc.) communicate awareness. When something is not clear, ask the interviewer for clarification.

- **Reflect on what the interviewer tells you** and indicate that you understand it:

  Interviewer: *"We're looking for people who can take over the project on their own and complete it with a minimum of direct supervision."*
  Candidate: *"I see you are willing to give people responsibility and authority. This was rare in some organizations where*

I've been associated. Could you give me a picture of how this works? How frequently would I need to report results to my manager?"

- **Relax.** Be yourself. Laugh or express amazement or surprise where appropriate. Overuse of slang, however, may create too casual an impression.

- **Elicit feedback.** *"Am I giving you the information you need?"* or *"Was that clear?"*

- **Be personable, but not overly familiar.** People want to know what interests and excites you, but be careful to avoid political or controversial social topics. If the interviewer is promoting more social chatter than is necessary, deftly steer the interview back on track with a question about the job.

Mirror, Mirror

You can build rapport with the interviewer by subtly mirroring his or her posture, tone, and statements. Mirroring is a technique of matching without imitating. The process encourages a harmonious exchange with the other person and shows that you are listening.

Pay attention to the body language of your interviewer. If she leans forward attentively while making some points, do that too. When she says, "We are very concerned that the department doesn't become too rigid," you could say: "I understand that you don't want the department to become rigid, and I would want to keep people working together flexibly." If your interviewer speaks in measured tones, you should pace yourself accordingly. (Once you have paced successfully, you can lead by slowly changing the tone or energy if you wish, but start by matching.) Keep the mirroring subtle; use a light touch.

If your body and voice tone are in harmony with the interviewer's style, communication is furthered. Don't get so carried away that you are mimicking her, but do stay conscious of nonverbal dynamics.

No Footprints on the Carpets

- **Talking too much.** Answer each question, putting yourself in a positive light, and then look to the interviewer to see if she wants more. Avoid long stories about yourself.

- **Being competitive with the interviewer.** There's a thin line between promoting and pushing your position.

   Threatening: "*I think I could get this situation shaped up very quickly and get everyone back on track.*"
   Nonthreatening: "*I believe I can help you make the changes you want.*"

- **Speaking negatively about past employers or others.** If the employer asks a question about policies you disagreed with in past jobs, you can say frankly, "*I don't think ____ was handled as well as it could have been.*" Don't dramatize the negative.

- **Expressing neediness.** Employers do not hire people because they need jobs.

   Needy: "*I really need to work for a company where I can learn more about the business.*"
   Helpful: "*I see a great opportunity for growth here and know I can support your goals while developing my own capability.*"

EMPLOYER INSIGHT

*"There's a funny dynamic I've noticed, and that's the tendency people have to give me reasons for **not** hiring them, although that's not their real intention. They express reservations about little problems that can be overcome—"I **think** I could learn to do that" or " I've never done that before, but I'm willing to try." I would advise them to accent the positive.*

Controlling the Interview

Your objective in controlling the interview is to show the interviewer you are a results-oriented person and to ensure that your presentation holds the interviewer's interest. Here are some methods to control the interview:

- **Have an agenda.** Know in advance what main points you want to convey.

- **Prepare an index card.** On one side, list five important things you want to make sure the employer learns about you, and on the other side list five powerful questions you want to ask. Refer to the card during the interview.

☞ To prepare your card, turn to the Interview Express Planner, Section E on page 76.

- **Step in when the interview seems to be going in the wrong direction.** An interviewer who talks too much about irrelevancies is wasting valuable time you need to convey your key selling points.

QUESTIONS TO USE TO BRING THE INTERVIEW BACK ON TRACK

"Do you mind if I ask you a few questions?"

"Could you please give me more specifics about the duties."

"What are the advantages of your products over the competition's?"

"May I go over my resume with you?"

"What additional information can I give you?"

"Which qualities or capabilities do you consider most important for this position?"

Be Outrageous

Organizations are constantly pressed for new solutions in almost every aspect of their business: in productivity, innovation, global solutions, increased quality control, customer service, personnel management. They will pay special attention to you if your commitment, imagination, and energy level can be directed to their larger needs or strategies.

- **If you know your field well,** you might detect some rigid or old-fashioned thinking. Without threatening, challenge the way the job is structured and suggest new ways of working that could be more productive.

- **If you've been out of work or between jobs too long,** or if you've taken time to rear a child or engage in some entrepreneurial activity that failed, do not hide behind ambiguous or apologetic language. Be proud of what you've done. Talk about your experience and how it could be helpful in the upcoming job.

- **If you've worked in an area different from your present job target or held one position too long,** point out how this filled a need at the time, but that now you are committed to moving ahead. No apology necessary.

Creating Vision

Your first goal is to project a picture of success and excitement in the mind of the interviewer. You want the interviewer to *see* you in the job getting it done in new ways.

Ask about the future with questions such as: *"How do you envision this department over the next three years?"* or *"Where do you see this department in the firm's future?"* or *"Given how quickly the industry is changing, what is your view of your future product line?"*

Looking Your Best

Your clothes, posture, grooming, attitude, voice level, etc., are often more revealing than your words. Dress as someone already successful in the job would dress for an important meeting.

If you are entering the job market for the first time, notice how people in organizations you visit are dressed. Review newspaper fashion supplements or business publications. Ask friends with good fashion sense how you can look your best.

PRESENTATION CHECKLIST

- Quality clothes that are cleaned and pressed and fit well
- Shoes that are polished, midheeled, preferably black
- A haircut within two weeks
- Manicured nails

- Minimal and discreet jewelry. Men: watches and wedding rings only; no necklaces, earrings, or ID bracelets. Women: no dangling earrings or clinking charm bracelets.
- Classic, not trendy, styles: not too sexy, not too plain
- Subtle perfume or aftershave
- Fabric: Stick with natural fibers—wool, silk, cotton
- Color: Wear power colors. Women: red, navy, gray, or black suits. Pastels are for out of office, and brown is out of the question. Men: navy blue or charcoal gray suits; white shirts; conservative ties.
- Hair and makeup: Keep your hair under control and out of your face. Makeup should be low-key.

Power Listening

The way you listen is part of the impression you make. Stay alert to what is directly expressed as well as to what is implied by the interviewer's manner and tone of voice.

TIPS FOR LISTENING

- In your pre-interview role plays, have your "employer/representative" prepare several eight-to-ten-line statements that might be made in an interview. Ask her to deliver them to you verbatim during the mock interview, stopping arbitrarily to ask you to repeat what's just been said as precisely as you can.
- As you listen make distinctions between statements and questions.

A **statement** puts forth information. Your responsibility is to understand and remember the facts that are given.

Interviewer: "*We want to hire people who have had direct experience with federal agencies.*"
You: "*I understand.*"

A **question** is a request for specific information.

Interviewer: "*Do you have experience with federal agencies?*"
You: "*Yes. I've worked closely with municipalities, and know this experience could be helpful to you..*"

- When listening, ask yourself: *"What's the main point?"* If you are having trouble discerning it, ask the speaker for clarification.

- Take quick, clear notes.

- Positive energy counts. However, Rachel Hott, communications trainer for the American Management Association, notes: "Don't jar people with your excitement; mirror their style first, and then lead them slowly to more enthusiasm or ask a provocative question. Don't assume that because a person is not expressing enthusiasm she isn't listening. Their way of saying yes might be subtle."

- Reduce social banter. If the socializing has gone on too long, ask a question that gets the interview back on track.

- Avoid arguments. If the employer says something you don't agree with, simply acknowledge the employer's position by saying: *"I understand how you feel about that."*

6

PAINTING A PICTURE
OF SUCCESS

Employers are in the business of hiring the right people, because a company is only as good as the people who do its work. The people they hire, their greatest resource, come from a pool of talent that includes you.

However, previous experience at school or in a job is not enough to convince an employer of your future success. Your task in an interview is to paint a picture of success in the mind of the interviewer.

This chapter describes how to project a dynamic image of yourself as a successful employee.

Universal Hiring Rule

Any employer will hire any individual if the employer is convinced that the hire will produce more value than it costs.

Convinced is the key word. No matter how extensive your background may be, the interviewer needs to see clearly that what you offer generates more value than it costs. The fundamental focus of the interview is on value.

This is true during times of recession, depression, high unemployment, or even layoffs in your industry.

Ten Ways to Create Value

- **Generate revenue:** introduce new products, new markets, new sales.
- **Cut costs:** reduce overhead, purchase intelligently, pare down unnecessary expenses.
- **Increase productivity:** develop more efficient work systems, training programs, service plans.

- **Be innovative**: gracefully challenge old models and traditional methods, improve packaging and design.
- **Improve quality**: enhance value to customers, reduce defects, promote shrewd inspection.
- **Save time**: improve work flow, organize delivery methods.
- **Focus on customers**: understand their needs, ensure customer satisfaction.
- **Use technology**: computerize, communicate with E mail and LAN, train employees to make technological leaps.
- **Motivate others**: get people to collaborate and cooperate.
- **Transform problems into opportunities**: focus on possibilities, redirect negative scrutiny to positive attention, open up new ways of thinking, being and doing.

Your Unique Selling Proposition

Articulating your singularity is easier when you know the company's particular needs and challenges. You can then make a convincing case for how your capabilities will enhance the employer's achievements and exceed the standard job requirements

SOME UNIQUE PROPOSITIONS

- You have worked on problems similar to those the employer faces, *and* from different perspectives.
- You have knowledge of a particular technology that can ease bottlenecks, reduce costs, and speed service.
- Your particular combination of training and experience makes you especially qualified to serve the employer's vision.
- You understand the competitive situation in detail.
- You have talked to customers and know their concerns.
- You comprehend underlying issues even better than those within the organization.
- Your qualitative self-assessment projects you far ahead of those with otherwise similar qualities (integrity, persistence, leadership, etc.).
- You thoroughly understand a particular market and could provide access to this market for the employer.
- You rise to a challenge and will not give up until it's met.

Strengthening Your Unique Selling Proposition

Asserting your uniqueness in terms the employer can understand strengthens your position, but present your strengths in an unthreatening way. Be careful not to downplay the efforts of the company. Offer an added solution.

☞ To prepare your unique selling proposition, turn to the Interview Express Planner, Section F on page 77.

Projecting Success

Present a specific and positive picture of what you can do. Use active words and phrases that make the invisible idea visible.

> *Nonvisual language:* "*I work according to a very high standard.*"
>
> *Visual language:* "*My high standards produce tangible results that* **look** *like this . . . Could we* **focus** *on the department's shift from local to global interests?. . . Let's* **picture** *markets across the world . . .*"

Include the interviewer in your visions of future success. Ask: "*As the department expands, how do you see your own job developing?*" or "*How would your consumers perceive this product?*" or "*With future product expansion, how do you see this department functioning?*"

Build a Future

Your interview will often focus on your history: "*What did you do in your last job?*" "*What are your proudest accomplishments?*" etc. Speak boldly of your future efforts as well.

Direct the conversation toward what can be created, not just what can be repeated. Speak in terms of possibility, opportunity, and foresight.

Accomplishments, Not Duties

In describing past work, make the distinction between accomplishments and duties. Duties are what your job *requires* you to do. Accomplishments are the *tangible results*. Anyone can perform a job's *duties*, but your *accomplishments* are unique.

POWER WORDS

When you speak about results you've produced, you paint a strong picture of success. Below is a list of active verbs that will clarify your descriptions of your accomplishments.

Increased	Decreased
Saved	Improved
Created	Changed
Solved	Built
Reduced	Won
Sold	Solved
Transformed	Developed
Initiated	

☞ To list your most relevant accomplishments, turn to the Interview Express Planner, Section G on page 78.

Projecting Personal Qualities

Given the rapid changes in technology, some of your skills will quickly become obsolete. Although you want to describe what qualifications you have now, you should stress leadership qualities that distinguish you from run-of-the-mill candidates.

BEST-SELLING LEADERSHIP QUALITIES

- Confidence in times of uncertainty
- Communication that effects action in others
- Innovativeness and versatility

- Ability to motivate others
- Concern for customers
- Orientation toward high quality, peak performance
- A healthy competitive edge
- Global thinking
- Skill in coordinating complex tasks
- Willingness to promote diversity

Which of these can you claim? Practice speaking about your leadership qualities.

☞ To list your best-selling leadership qualities, turn to the Interview Express Planner, Section H on page 79.

EMPLOYER INSIGHTS

"The pace of business is much faster than ever before. We need people who are versatile, who can jump into a new project at a moment's notice, stay on top of the changes in technology, and who can basically reengineer their job with little supervision."

Reinventing the Job

Expand the employer's thinking about the position he's offering. Keep in mind that even with a clearly printed job description, the work is subject to interpretation, emphasis, and change.

Here are some questions to expand the interviewer's thoughts about a job. Create others on your own:

"How can the job be done more efficiently and at lower cost?"

"What would make the workplace more stimulating?"

"How can we coach others to attain higher levels of performance and satisfaction?"

"How can products and services be improved?"

"What are new ways to surprise and attract customers?"

"How can we identify undiscovered customer needs?"

"What would a breakthrough look like?"

To reinvent the job, turn to the Interview Express Planner, Section I on page 80.

How Are You Doing?

Eliciting your interviewer's reaction to your performance takes the spotlight off you for a moment and gives you time to regroup. Ask questions like these:

"On the basis of what you've heard so far, do you believe I have the qualifications you're looking for?"

"Would you like to hear more about my experience with_____?"

"I could give you more detail about my last assignment. Would that be useful?"

Negative response from an employer is a gift when you take it as constructive criticism and respond appropriately. Unstated reservations leave you powerless to remedy the situation.

Turn negative comments around with questions such as:

"I appreciate your response. If I were able to improve that significantly, would I be eligible?"

"I appreciate your frankness. If you were me, what would you do to rise above the norm?"

"I understand how it could be a problem. I can overcome that and would be glad to work with you on it."

"I appreciate your feedback and know several ways to strengthen my knowledge of that (process, product, etc.). Can we still consider the opportunity open?"

7

PROVING YOUR POINT

You've painted a picture of success. The employer has listened to you, seems interested in the possibilities you offer, and now challenges you to defend your statements, to be more specific about your claims. Now it's time to build your case so that the interviewer feels comfortable making you an offer.

There's Only One Question

The one question underlying the hiring process is: *Why should I hire you?* When the employer asks, *"Tell me about your experience,"* she means, *"Why should I hire you?"*

What Employers Want to Know

1. **If I put you on the job, what will the results be?** Is your combination of competency, will, and responsibility sufficient to produce the outcome this job demands?

2. **How long will it take for you to become productive?** Do you learn quickly, what do you already know, and how much time will it take to get you started?

3. **How much supervision will you need?** The less the better. Most managers prefer that *you* supply them with ideas rather than the other way around.

4. **Do you generate more value than you cost?** Even though the job may be routine in procedure, employers like to know you are a valuable person and can reduce costs and generate benefits.

5. **Could you be a high performer?** Will you exceed the requirements of the job description? Are you competitive? Do you like to win and help others win?

6. **Will you fit into the culture?** Will other employees be comfortable with you? Will you enhance the smooth running of the operation? If you create turbulence, will it be positive?

7. **Will you be fun to work with?** You will be considered a great asset if you can smile and laugh *and* get the job done.

8. **Are you responsible?** Are you accountable for your actions and their results? Responsibility is an attitude, not just a job assignment.

9. **Can you manage your own development?** Employers look for people who are self-starters and able to manage their own future and seek out new skills and responsibilities.

10. **Will you stay?** Can you be counted on to sustain your energy and commitment through rough periods? If you accept the job, will it be for reasons above and beyond personal survival needs?

There's Only One Answer

The best answer to the question *"Why should I hire you?"* stems from the Universal Hiring Rule: **Any employer will hire any individual if the employer is convinced that the hire will produce more value than it costs.**

REASONS AN EMPLOYER SHOULD HIRE YOU

1. **You will create consistent and measurable value on the job.**

2. **Your past accomplishments indicate you are able to do the job.** The employer is not buying motivation alone. She wants to see quantifiable demonstrations of your talents in your job history. Can you quantify what you've done?

3. **You are a fast learner.**

4. **You are committed.** A committed person gets the work done and is not deterred by obstacles.

5. **You are versatile and flexible.** Departments change, politics change, technologies change, businesses change. Your ability to adapt creatively is a powerful asset.

Fielding Questions

The interview is a conversational dance of questions. Anticipating questions will prepare you for them.

OPEN QUESTIONS

An open question is a general request for information. For example, questions like *"Tell me about your experience in telemarketing"* or *"Where do you see yourself going in advertising?"* give you an opportunity to relate your past to the future. Be assertive about what you can contribute.

CLOSED QUESTIONS

A closed question calls for a yes/no or highly focused response. Examples: *"Can you work under pressure?"* *"Did you have your own budget?"* and *"Were you given authority to change the plans?"* Don't avoid a negative response. If asked, *"Did you ever work on the XR7G multiprocessor?"* don't weakly answer, *"I've worked on machines like it and heard a lot about it."* Answer forthrightly: *"No, I haven't. However, I've worked on similar machines and am a fast learner."* Such directness, followed by a positive message, gives a strong impression.

PROBE QUESTIONS

A probe question is designed to elicit further information or to double-check for consistency. If you say you managed the West Side offices, the employer may ask: *"How many people did you manage?"* followed by *"Were they all full-time employees?"* or *"What size budget did you directly control?"*

QUESTIONING THE QUESTION

If the employer's question is too broad—*"Tell me about yourself"*—narrow it down in your favor: *"What would you most like to hear about?"* If you are not sure what the "real" question is, ask.

Employer: "Do you think you could work in this kind of environment?"

You: "Are you referring to technical expertise or personality?"

LEADING QUESTIONS

A leading question "telegraphs" the desired answer:

Employer: "I don't imagine you'd have any problem writing proposals like this, would you?"

You: "Not at all."

It's fair to take advantage of leading questions, but you can make a bigger impression if you add something to the expected response. For example:

You: "I've had lots of experience with proposals and it would be no problem. Tell me more about the proposals you prepare."

Leading questions can reveal the interviewer's bias for or against you. Listen carefully; accentuate the positive, eliminate the negative.

POSITIVE LEADS

"How well do you work under pressure?"

"I don't suppose you'd have any trouble managing four or five people in different locations, would you?"

NEGATIVE LEADS

"Don't you think this work might be more complex than your past job?" (*You:* "Yes. I thrive on complexity.")

"Won't it be difficult for you to manage five older men?" (*You:* "I know it won't be too difficult for me. How do you think they'll respond?")

Use leading questions to provide fresh evidence that you are the right person for the job.

I'M SORRY, I DON'T KNOW

If the assumption in a leading question is not true, say so directly.

Employer: "I suppose you've had fairly good experience on MS-DOS computers . . ."

You: "No, I really haven't. My last job called for Macintosh, but I'm committed and look forward to learning DOS."

- Make sure you understand a question before you answer it.
- If a question is complex or challenging, take time to think about it. Say: *"I need to think about that for a minute."*
- Quantify your answers when possible. (*"I managed a telemarketing staff of twenty-five people and increased sales by thirty-five percent."*)
- After you answer a question, find out if the employer heard what you intended to communicate. *"Did that answer your question?"*
- Be willing to challenge an interviewer's assumptions. *"I don't agree that a master's degree is essential for that work."*
- Know when you've said enough. Stimulate interest without draining attention. Ask: *"Would you like to hear more about that?"*

EMPLOYER INSIGHTS

"There is a time in most interviews for straight questions and answers. I like applicants, however, who engage me in conversation and take the initiative. I often learn more about the applicant from the questions she asks than from the answers she gives."

Test Questions

Here are twenty questions frequently used in interviews. Some may or may not apply to your current situation. Think through your answers or write them down.

1. Tell me about yourself.

Suggestion: For the world's most wide-open question, your best response might be, *"That's a big assignment. Let me briefly outline the things I've done that I think are relevant to this job opening."*

2. Why are you interested in our company?

Suggestion: Include what you know about the firm. *"From*

what I've learned so far about your approach to customers, I know I can make a contribution to Abex and be challenged to grow."

3. **Why are you interested in this position?**

    Suggestion: See above. It's advantageous to know about the job before the interview. If you don't, early in the interview ask: *"I have very general information about the job. I wonder if you could give me some more detail?"*

4. **Where do you see yourself going?**

    Suggestion: Be concrete. Try: *"I'd like to expand my ability to solve technical problems for customers."*

5. **What special qualities do you bring to this job?**

    Suggestion: Make distinctions between qualities and skills. Emphasize your unique qualities as well as those widely held (ability to learn, creativity, imagination, leadership, etc.).

6. **What are your greatest strengths?**

    Suggestion: Respond by describing those strengths that correspond to what the employer is looking for.

7. **What are your greatest weaknesses?**

    Suggestion: Emphasize what you are honestly working on and improving. *"I am working on improving my ability to prepare formal proposals."*

8. **Do you perform well under pressure?**

    Suggestion: The obvious answer is *"Very well."* To take greatest advantage of the lead, ask what kind of pressure there is and focus your answer on the response to that question. This will also give you a better picture of the job.

9. **Do you prefer to work on your own or with others?**

    Suggestion: *"I have no problem with either, depending on what needs to get done."*

10. **I see that you majored in liberal arts. Did you take any business courses?**

    Suggestion: Only narrow thinkers insist that the major field of study should match the job. A liberal arts background can be applied to business when refocused. Try this: *"Yes, I did. I enjoyed the business courses I took and did well in them. Also, given the rapid changes in global business, a strong historical perspective from my liberal arts work should be very useful."*

11. **I see you finished only three years of college. Do you plan to complete your degree work?**

Suggestion: Often you'll need to override a bias that a degree confirms success on the job. Counter with this: *"You're looking for someone with a degree. I understand that. I left college for financial reasons and found that my work experience served me well and will help me to learn a job more efficiently and effectively. Once I settle into the new position, I'll complete my degree, focusing on courses that will be most useful to this job."*

12. **Tell me about your extracurricular activities.**

Suggestion: Mention any activities where developed skills and qualities could be useful at work (resolving conflict, organizing projects, budgeting, teamwork, etc.). If you had few or no extracurricular activities, you could say: *"Most of my time outside class was spent supporting school expenses. This experience has helped me build a practical approach that will be useful in this job."*

13. **I see that you finished around the middle of your class.**

Suggestion: To respond to a less than average performance, say, *"My grades were not what they could have been. Those were years of change, and it took me a while to organize myself in an unfamiliar environment. Though my grades were low, I now know what it takes to get a job done. I can make a major impact in this job and will surprise you with the results."*

14. **Tell me about your last job.**

Suggestion: Emphasize the relationship between your past accomplishments and duties and the responsibilities of the prospective job. Stress accomplishments more than the duties required of you.

15. **Why did you leave your last job?**

Suggestion: This is a key question. If you left involuntarily: *"The work did not use my best strength, which is working with people. My mistake was that I didn't remedy the situation before they did."* If you left or are leaving your last job voluntarily, try something like this: *"I liked the job and the people; however, I'm interested in a job that allows me to make a bigger contribution, which is why I'm talking to you."*

16. **What were your biggest accomplishments in your last job?**

    Suggestion: Be prepared to answer with results you *produced* rather than duties you were given. Point out specific items from your resume.

17. **How would your last boss describe you?**

    Suggestion: If your performance was excellent: *"She is eager to recommend me, although sorry to see me go. Please call her."* If there was a problem: *"The relationship could have been better. My boss was a good manager, but we had different ideas about getting the job done. If you'd like a reference, contact ____"* and name a person you know will evaluate you favorably.

18. **Looking back at your last job, where do you think your performance could have been improved?**

    Suggestion: Even though you did well, look at where you could have sought greater responsibility and results. Apply this to what you can do in the future.

19. **What are your long-term goals?**

    Suggestion: Today organizations prefer employees to make continuous improvement in the quality and scope of their work rather than take rigid steps up an organizational ladder. Speak about expanding the range of things you can do, learn, and apply.

20. **Are you interviewing with other companies?**

    Suggestion: Let your interviewer know you are competitive and have other opportunities. The wrong answer would be to say, *"No, this is the only place I'm looking."* A better answer: *"I am looking at several different opportunities. What I see here so far looks good."*

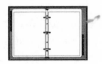

☞ To anticipate questions that could come up in your interview, turn to the Interview Express Planner, Section J on page 82.

GETTING OUT OF TOUGH SPOTS

- **If the interviewer is looking for skills or experience you don't have,** you might say: *"I don't believe this is a shortcoming. I* *know I could learn ____ quickly with the right training. The other qualities I bring to the job may be even more useful."*

- **If the interviewer implies or says you don't have the right education:** *"I know how important a master's degree might seem. However, I'm confident my practical experience [give examples] will more than compensate for the lack of a degree. Would you be willing to give me ninety days on the job to prove it?"*

- **If you don't think you've done well at the interview,** call back: *"Frankly, I don't believe I was very effective in my interview yesterday. I was nervous and distracted. May I come back tomorrow or later in the week to give you a half hour of my best? You will discover I have something quite useful to offer."*

Out of Bounds

Discriminatory practices in the workplace have been significantly reduced through both legislation and changing attitudes. However, discrimination is still an important issue, especially if you are its victim. If you believe you have been unfairly treated, contact your local Department of Labor for advice.

The following areas of inquiry are out of bounds in an interview:

- Race, ethnic background, or national origin
- Religious affiliation
- Marital status
- Family makeup: names or ages of dependents
- Gender and, in some states and municipalities, sexual orientation
- Social clubs or organizations
- Age (unless required by the job)
- Weight or height
- Arrest record

ALTERNATIVE ACTIONS

Options you have if you are asked questions you consider discriminatory:

1. Consider the spoken question and the underlying question from

the interviewer's standpoint. Respond in a way that answers the employer's concerns.

Employer: "Do you have children?"
You: "Yes, I have two school-age boys and we have full-time child care."

2. Ask how the information is relevant to the position.
3. Politely inform the interviewer that you think the question may be discriminatory and you'd prefer not to answer it.

Sometimes interviewers will ask questions that have unintended discriminatory effects. We recommend that you avoid "going legal" or confronting this at the interview unless you see an obvious pattern. If a discriminatory pattern is clearly developing and it looks as if it could be harmful to your chances of getting the offer, you have the choice of raising the issue then and thereby asking to meet with someone else in the firm such as the Human Resources Director, or waiting until after the interview and confronting the situation if you don't get an offer.

In either case, discreetly make detailed notes during the interview or immediately after it of the exact questions that were asked.

8

CLOSING IN ON THE OFFER

You are approaching pay dirt. Assuming the job interests you and you interest the employer, it's time to sharpen your focus on the endgame.

I'm Sorry, but . . .

The closer the employer gets to making an offer, the more prominent his or her doubts will become.

An objection is not a rejection; it's simply an obstacle to overcome. Unfortunately, objections can momentarily knock the wind out of your sails, weakening your will to continue. You may say to yourself: *"I didn't want that job anyway!"*

A negative reaction to a valid objection can create a self-fulfilling prophecy: You get discouraged and lose interest, the employer then loses interest, and momentum is lost. The best approach to an objection is to hear it as an indication that you're under consideration.

Objections reflect the "I'd like to hire you, but . . ." phase. Realize that what is before the "but"—"I'd like to hire you"—is as important as what follows it. In your mind's ear change the interviewer's *but* to *and*: *"I'd like to hire you and you don't have the degree we're looking for."* If you drop the negative connotation of the word *but* and replace it with the positive power of *and,* you will be in a better position to make the necessary leap to get the offer.

Overcoming Objections

- **Anticipate objections**. Write them down. "I'd like to hire you, but (and) . . ." Rehearse until you're comfortable with your rebuttal.

- When you hear an objection, **acknowledge the speaker's concerns.** For example: ***Employer:*** *(I'd like to hire you, but ...)* *"We're not hiring right now."*

  You: *"I can understand that, given the economy..."*

- After you've acknowledged the validity of the objection, **offer a way to overcome it.** *"On the other hand, I have some unique capabilities and could make an immediate contribution to your marketing."*

- **Push for a decision.** *"I'm available now, but not indefinitely. I think if we got together soon, the benefits would show up in a few months. Would it be possible to make a decision in the next week?"*

HOW WOULD YOU RESPOND
TO THESE OBJECTIONS?

(Remember to use "I'd like to hire you, ~~but~~ and . . .")

1. We've received many top-notch candidates for this job and it will take some time to sort through them.

2. We'll get back to you.

3. You don't have the kind of experience we're looking for.

4. Unfortunately, we need someone with a degree in _____ for this job.

5. You're overqualified.

6. We've had a change of plans and are going to postpone hiring.

Suggestions for Handling
Some Common Objections

1. **We've received many top-notch candidates for this job and it will take some time to sort through them.**

   Suggestion: Try *"Congratulations! The job deserves a top-notch candidate and I see why many are attracted to it. I offer some unique qualities and also need to come to my own decision shortly. Perhaps it would be useful to meet and start a conversation, so we'd be prepared to move quickly."*

2. **We'll get back to you.**

   Suggestion: Try to obtain a commitment to the next step. *"I appreciate the time it takes to make decisions. Do you think my qualifications will satisfy your needs?"* If so, *"Can we schedule the next meeting now?"* or *"Who is the next person I need to meet to get closer to a final decision?"* If your qualifications do not satisfy, you might ask: *"What would I have to show you to enhance my standing?"*

3. You don't have the kind of experience we're looking for.

Suggestion: *"I can understand why you'd want someone with direct experience in . . . On the other hand, my experience, particularly since it is nontraditional, would provide beneficial new perspectives in today's fast-changing climate."*

4. Unfortunately, we need someone with a degree in _____ for this job.

Suggestion: This is similar to objections about not having the "right" experience. You need to understand why a company is looking for a particular degree or background. You might ask: *"Would it be possible to hire a good person who doesn't have the exact degree and train him to do the job your way?"* Help the company rethink the job and consider alternatives.

5. You're overqualified.

Suggestion: This is one of the more difficult objections to understand. It usually reflects the employer's assumption that you'll want more than he can pay. Explore with a question or two: *"Are you concerned about compensation?"* or *"If I could make a significant reduction in the cost of operations, would you be willing to discuss the situation further?"*

6. We've had a change of plans and are going to postpone hiring.

Suggestion: This objection is frequent in tenuous economic times. The best response could be to offer alternatives to full-time work. You might be willing to start as an independent consultant for a few months. This relieves the employer of having to make a full-time commitment until ready.

☞ To plan how you will overcome possible objections, turn to the Interview Express Planner, Section K on page 83.

Closing Moments

As you close the interview, you'll want to find out how well you've been received, when the next interview will be, how and when a decision will be made, and, most of all, if you're in line for an offer.

FOUR CLOSING STRATEGIES

1. Recap the benefits you offer.

"Let me reiterate how I see this job and how I could help..." or *"You said you want someone who can accomplish.... My (training, education, experience) over the last few years will enable me to do this for you. What's the next step toward a final decision?"*

2. Make a proposition.

If you're interested in the job, give the employer an opportunity to say yes on the spot. *"Based on what I know about the job, I could give you what you want and more. I've got some ideas about starting on a provisional basis for maybe six months and if all goes well, we could negotiate a full-time position after that."*

3. Sow seeds for further discussion.

If you are not fully certain this is the job for you (you may have other offers pending) and want to continue to explore it, try this: *"This has been a very interesting meeting. I've learned a lot about where you are going. I think you have a full understanding of my capabilities. I'd like to take (a week) to think things over. Can we talk again Friday?"*

4. Push for a decision.

Try something like *"You said the decision comes from Mrs. Burns, the department manager. I wonder if it would be possible for me to meet her today or tomorrow. Can you check her schedule?"*

Follow-up Express

The memory of your outstanding interview quickly fades in the interviewer's mind unless you take action to reinforce its impact. Here's how:

- **Act now!** As soon as the interview is over, find a quiet place to sit and write:

___ Interviewer's name, company, division, time, date, and length of interview.

___ Key points you made and the interviewer's reactions.

___ Most important aspects of the job as presented by the interviewer.

___ The interviewer's key concerns and how you responded to them.

___ Next steps to take.

___ Things you wish you'd said, but didn't.

___ Things you said, but wish you hadn't.

___ Five or six actions you can take to follow up.

- **Get a letter into the interviewer's hands within forty-eight hours.** Yes, forty-eight hours—express mail or fax a one-page letter that reiterates your key propositions, how they relate to the job, what you think the next steps should be. Make it interesting and relevant. You will stand out positively in the employer's memory if the letter is both a thank-you and a recap.

EMPLOYER INSIGHTS

"I often get letters from people after the interview, and of the ones that come in, most are simple one-paragraph thank-you notes. What really makes an impression on me is a letter that tells me something new or challenges my thinking."

- **Answer open questions.** If a topic from a previous conversation remains unresolved, jot a note to your interviewer expressing your thoughts "upon reflection." If there were some areas in your presentation you felt were weak or wanting, offer reinforcement in a letter or telephone call.

- **Reportage.** Look for articles in newspapers and trade journals to support positions you took. Highlight relevant points of interest and send a copy to your interviewer with the notation "For Your Information" with your name or card.

- **Make the best of the worst.** If you'd like to forget about an embarrassing interview, don't. Use the next day or two to reassert your self-confidence. Then call back, admit you could have done better, and request a second chance. This *could* lead to another interview. Even if it does not, congratulate yourself for being bold enough to take a stab at it.

- **Plant a seed.** With each of your follow-up efforts, plant a seed that will reap positive events. You might say: *"Let's meet again and discuss these issues..."* or *"I look forward to talking to you again soon to see what our next steps will be."*

One Week Later

Have a follow-up conversation with the interviewer five to six business days after your first meeting. Don't assume your forty-eight-hour letter or fax was received. Call to confirm it and set up a second meeting while you're at it.

STRATEGIES FOR THE FIRST WEEK'S FOLLOW-UP

- **Come up with a question that justifies a call.** For example: *"Helen, this is Jane Newman; we met last week. Did you get the article I sent you? As I reviewed my notes, I had a question about how the job relates to foreign subsidiaries. Do you have a few minutes to talk about that?"* or *"I've been thinking about our discussions on the direction of your department and how it relates to the job we've been talking about. Could we meet for fifteen or twenty minutes to go over some questions I have?"*

- **Clear the calendar.** *"Jim, you mentioned the next step is to see Becky Bellinger, the group head. I've got a couple of dates available at the end of next week. Should we try to get on her calendar soon?"*

- **Squeeze play.** Hint that you have other employers interested in you. It's dangerous, but has been known to work. Tread carefully: *"Jim, I don't want to press my luck just because I've got several potential employers interested but, naturally, I'd like to accelerate our meetings so our opportunity to work together does not slip by."*

Weekly Checkups

Try to make sure that no more than three weeks pass between the first and second interviews. If more time than that goes by, a longer-term follow-up is required. (See below.)

The secret to maintaining a pace is to contact the employer at least every ten days. Send a note or news item of interest or phone in. *"Jim, it's Nancy Davis. Is it time to set up the second meeting we talked about?"* or *"Can we meet next week to continue our conversation?"* Start referring to your interview as a "meeting" or "conversation" to keep things informal.

If several weeks go by and you are not getting anywhere, make a more specific request. *"I'd like to see if we could set a date for our next meeting because I'm making some decisions. Can we meet next Tuesday or Wednesday?"*

Longer-term Follow-up

If you're still interested and nothing happens in four weeks to let you know you're under consideration, try putting the idea out of your mind for another four weeks. At this point (eight or so weeks after the interview), push for another meeting. You don't want to seem overeager after the lull, but on the other hand, you want to know if the opportunity still exists. *"Jim, I've been preoccupied with some other projects, but now that they're finished, I'd like to meet to continue our earlier conversation."*

9
GOING FOR THE GOLD

While we work for love and personal fulfillment, most of us need incentives to perform at our best. This chapter describes how to move away from a "take what you get" mentality toward one of "have what you want." This shift involves making the most of what you deliver to the employer and what compensation they give you in return.

Money Follows Value

A fundamental rule about money is: To earn more money, you must produce more value (turn a department around, create the best ad, eliminate two steps in the production process, convince the big customers to come your way). This is when money starts to flow.

Money Isn't All of It

In considering what you are paid, you must consider total compensation. Although many items in the compensation package may not be negotiable (e.g., the employer's health plan, work schedule, etc.), these benefits should be considered when you tally up the offer. For example, a company may offer you a higher salary but fewer benefits, so when everything is considered, you could be making twenty percent less.

Components of a total compensation package to consider include:

- Insurance: health, dental, optical, life, accidental death, workmen's comp, disability
- Bonuses and profit sharing
- Stock options
- Paid sick leave, maternity leave, emergency leave

- Pension plans
- Educational and training allowances
- Memberships
- Company car, car allowance, parking space
- Relocation package
- Discounts
- Job discontinuation policy

Soft-Edged Compensation

In addition to the more tangible aspects of a compensation package listed above, there are other less obvious ones that are being negotiated by an increasing number of employers. These include work scheduling, adjusting hours to fit child rearing or educational needs, planning sabbaticals for leave with/without pay, doing part of your job at a home computer with a modem, or job sharing.

These "soft benefits" can also include opportunities to upgrade your skills and capabilities. Many companies are reputed for their career development and training programs; working for such a company can help you move toward your career goals. Look for companies with a strong commitment to developing their people through formal training programs, tuition reimbursement policies, on-the-job training, and personal coaching.

Fast-Track Companies

Some companies are definitely on a fast track, growing rapidly at the forefront of an expanding industry. In a small, growing firm, you may start at a lower salary and compensation package, but as the company expands, your role and salary will expand along with it. On the other hand, the company could falter and decline, so there's a risk to consider.

More Is Better

We know compensation is not everything. Personal satisfaction and self-expression are enormously important. Making more money does not ensure greater satisfaction in life. People can be as dissatisfied with seven-figure incomes as with five-figure incomes.

At a higher salary, however, you will usually have more interesting work and stiffer challenges. Continue to do everything you can to increase compensation to the top ranks in your field; both the standard of living and quality of your working life will be improved.

Building Earning Power

- Think value. Describe your capabilities in terms of the value they can provide the organization. "I understand the contracting process thoroughly. I see some areas where we can increase the profitability of our contracts and the way we position our services."

- Speak about the results you know you will produce for the employer. Don't allow your previous low income to limit your expectations.

- Continue to expand your capabilities by taking courses, reading books and articles in the field, getting close to people who are recognized in the field. This ongoing process of self-improvement translates into future bargaining power.

- Be willing to take on more responsibility.

- Talk accomplishments, not duties. "At the APEX Company, I led a team that reduced quality defects from an average of 750 per vehicle to 100 per vehicle. If I'd stayed there longer, I'm sure we could have brought it down close to zero."

Negotiate

Don't settle for what's being offered. Your willingness and ability to negotiate for yourself demonstrates your personal effectiveness.

There are a few risks in negotiating. Your requests may exceed the employer's resources, or the employer may have a smaller picture of the possibilities in the job than you do, and someone else might be chosen. But more often a higher salary is won. Don't cave in to what you know is a low offer.

Build your case in advance.

- Know what you can deliver in tangible terms. Write it down.

- Investigate current salary ranges in your field using salary surveys prepared by the College Placement Council for entry-level jobs or using earning figures published by the Department of

Labor. Scan classified ads in newspapers from around the country to see what salaries are advertised in your field. Check with trade associations and seek out people who are established in the field and ask their opinions. Consult with executive search firms and placement agencies.

- Know the competition. Talk to other companies to determine what the current salary ranges are.

- Know your strengths. Steer the conversation toward what you can do better than others.

Negotiating Strategies

1. **Let the employer name the salary figure first.**

   Never answer the question *"What is the minimum salary you would accept?"* Respond by saying: *"Frankly, I'm not looking for the minimum. I expect that I'll receive two or three offers before I decide, and I will probably take the offer that gives me the best opportunity to make a contribution and the best salary. What salary range are you offering?"*

2. **When a salary range is presented, acknowledge the top of the range.**

   Employer: "The range for this job is $25,000 to $30,000 per year." *You:* "Thirty thousand seems in the ballpark."

EMPLOYER INSIGHTS

"I'd rather pay more for the best candidate than settle for someone who is willing to accept a lower salary range. We have too much invested to go bargain hunting."

---

3. **Give value to what you offer whenever you are speaking of salary.**

   Emphasize your contributions: working better, reducing costs, increasing margins, etc. Avoid talking about your needs and obligations.

4. **Negotiate for the future, not from the past.**

   When the employer asks, "What did you make on your last job?" and you feel it's not relevant to what you want from this job, say something like: *"In my last job I was paid below the* market price for my skills. I was willing to accept this for a while because it gave me the opportunity to learn and develop; now I am very clear about the value I can offer to an employer and I want my salary to be competitive."

5. **Never accept an offer at the time that it's given.**

You may be tempted to breathe a sigh of relief and accept the first offer. Don't. When an offer is made, take a deep breath and say, *"Thank you for the offer. I know I can make a contribution to this job. I need to take a few days to consider this offer in light of my future plans. Can I get back to you next Tuesday?"* By showing that *you* are going to make the decision, you change the game entirely. The employer is now waiting for you to accept him, which gives you a psychological advantage. The employer might respond that she needs an answer sooner. You can negotiate the time frame, but under no circumstances should you accept the job at the moment the offer is made.

6. **Consider the offer and then get back to the negotiation.**

Take the time to decide whether this is the job you want and whether the salary is commensurate with what you need. If you decide you want the job, call the employer to see if you can boost the offer. *"I've been considering your offer and appreciate it. My target for this job has always been $30,000 per year, and I wonder if you could match that number?"* The employer may object or defer the decision. Just listen and hold to your position.

Salary negotiation is naturally uncomfortable. There may be moments when you think you might have gone too far. Check it out without apology: *"Is this within the budget?"* If you haven't turned the offer down, you can backtrack: *"I do understand that you were unable to raise the salary figure. Would you be willing after ninety days to review the salary?"*

7. **If it's not going to happen, find out soon.**

If the negotiation is going nowhere, ask questions to move it along. **You:** *"What would I have to be able to do to be worth $35,000 a year to your company?"* **Employer:** *"I can't think of any way that you could make that as a starting salary."* **You:** *"I appreciate your frankness. I really do need to take another day to consider whether I'm able to accept the job."*

8. **Don't fall for the line "I'm sorry; the salary ranges are set by**

corporate policy" if you think there is room to negotiate.

You: "Is there someone else to whom I could speak to nego-tiate the salary, or is there another suitable job in a higher salary range?"

9. Make sure that both sides win.

Negotiations should never be angry or emotional, no matter how much pressure there is on either side. Assert your value so that the employer will view you as a highly worthwhile addi-tion rather than someone who is overpriced.

☞ To plan your negotiations strategy, turn to the Interview Express Planner, Section L on page 84.

10
FINAL PREPARATION

Practice with Role Playing

The interview is the main event. It is not the time to practice your questions and answers. Practice a few days before the interview. The better the rehearsal, the better your performance.

Find someone, preferably with a background similar to the prospective interviewer's, who can take an hour to role-play an interview. If you can't find anyone in your job target field, ask a career counselor or someone with supervisory experience. If all else fails ask a friend or family member.

Brief the person playing the role of the interviewer. Have that person read your resume and a list of the questions you expect will be asked in the actual interview. (See the sample questions in Chapter 7.)

If you can, videotape your role-play or ask a third person to be an observer. This person should be prepared to comment on the impression you make, your body language, your enthusiasm and interest, and the content of your answers.

Enter the room and greet the "interviewer" as you would in real life. The role-playing interviewer should conduct the interview as authentically as possible. Don't break out of the scene to make comments. Answer the questions. Ask your own whether or not the role-play interviewer knows the correct response.

After the role-play ask the observer and interviewer to critique your performance. Don't defend, explain, or justify your actions. Listen to the feedback and take notes.

Practice the role-play two or three times with variations. Switch roles in one. You can gain valuable insights by asking the questions and listening to how someone else's answers impress you.

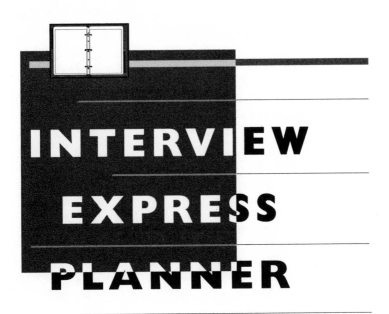

INTERVIEW EXPRESS PLANNER

Make copies of these forms.
Complete them in advance of each interview.

SECTION A: VISUALIZATION OF FUTURE SUCCESS

(Chapter 1, page 5) Picture yourself already working on the job, being productive and successful. See the value you are creating and the impact you make.

What does your workspace look like? _____

_____

_____

What are you doing? _____

_____

_____

What type of people do you work with and for? _____

_____

_____

What results have you produced in the last six months? _____

_____

_____

What capabilities have you developed from working in this job?

_____

_____

What interests you most about this job? _____

_____

_____

SECTION B:
NETWORK CONTACTS

(Chapter 2, page 10) List the people you know (or would like to know) who can help you reach a decision maker for the job you are interviewing for.

Name: _____

Address: _____

Phone: _____

Ways to help: _____

Name: _____

Address: _____

Phone: _____

Ways to help: _____

Name: _____

Address: _____

Phone: _____

Ways to help: _____

Name: _____

Address: _____

Phone: _____

Ways to help: _____

Name: _____

Address: _____

Phone: _____

Ways to help: _____

SECTION C:
YOUR TELEPHONE MESSAGE

(Chapter 2, page 13) Answer the following questions to organize your telephone presentation.

What points do you want to make? _____

_____

_____

_____

_____

Why would the prospective employer want to speak to you? (What would be valuable to the employer?) _____

_____

_____

_____

_____

What action(s) do you want to see happen as a result of this phone call? _____

_____

_____

_____

What is your specific request? _____

_____

_____

_____

What is your opening line? _____

_____

_____

SECTION D:
EMPLOYER RESEARCH

(Chapter 3, page 18) In advance of the interview, research and answer the following:

ABOUT THE COMPANY

Company/organization name: _____

What does it do? (products and services)_____

_____

_____

What is its mission? _____

_____

_____

What are the company's strategic objectives? _____

_____

_____

What has the company done? _____

_____

_____

Where is it headed?_____

_____

_____

What is the competition? _____

_____

_____

What factors influence the company's success _____

_____

_____

What are the company's current problems, challenges, and
changes? _____

_____

_____

What are the company's values? _____

_____

_____

ABOUT THE JOB

Your job target: _____

Interview is with: _____

Secretary's name (if you have it): _____

Division or department: _____

Address of interview (directions to get there): _____

_____

_____

Phone: _____

Description of position applied for: _____

_____

_____

_____

_____

Salary range: _____

How can the job contribute to the company's success? _____

_____

_____

_____

SECTION E: MY INTERVIEW AGENDA

(Chapter 5, page 33) Plan your agenda for the interview by answering the following. Prepare an index card to refer to during the interview.

List five important things you want to make sure the employer learns about you.

1. _____

2. _____

3. _____

4. _____

5. _____

List five powerful questions you want to ask during the interview.

1. _____

2. _____

3. _____

4. _____

5. _____

SECTION F: MY UNIQUE SELLING PROPOSITION

(Chapter 6, page 39) As you answer the next two questions, remember the Universal Hiring Rule: *Any employer will hire any individual if the employer is convinced that the hire will produce more value than it costs.*

Describe three specific ways in which you can contribute to the company's success.

1. _____

_____

2. _____

_____

3. _____

_____

How can you offer far more value than is required by the job description?

_____

_____

_____

_____

_____

_____

SECTION G: MY RELEVANT ACCOMPLISHMENTS

(Chapter 6, page 40) Describe five specific things you have done that demonstrate how you can contribute to the company's success. Do not describe past duties; explain the results you have produced.

1. _____

_____

2. _____

_____

3. _____

_____

4. _____

_____

5. _____

_____

SECTION H:
MY LEADERSHIP QUALITIES

(Chapter 6, page 41) What are your three most significant leadership qualities? Cite a past situation or accomplishment that demonstrates each quality.

Leadership quality: _____

Demonstration of this quality: _____

_____

_____

Leadership quality: _____

Demonstration of this quality: _____

_____

_____

Leadership quality: _____

Demonstration of this quality: _____

_____

_____

SECTION I:
A NEW LOOK AT THE JOB

(Chapter 6, page 42) Think about ways in which you can expand the employer's thinking about the position. Answer the following questions:

What would a breakthrough look like in how the job is done?

_____

_____

_____

_____

_____

What are some innovations in technology, training, etc., that the employer should consider for the job in the future? _____

_____

_____

_____

_____

_____

What could be done to accomplish the the job more efficiently or at a lower cost? _____

_____

_____

_____

_____

_____

How can the job more actively serve the company's customers?

_____

_____

_____

_____

_____

What can you do to motivate others to attain a higher level of performance and satisfaction? _____

_____

_____

_____

_____

_____

What would a breakthrough look like in how the job is done?

_____

_____

_____

_____

_____

SECTION J:
ANTICIPATED QUESTIONS

(Chapter 7, page 50) List five questions that you anticipate being asked in the interview:

1. _____
   _____

2. _____
   _____

3. _____
   _____

4. _____
   _____

5. _____
   _____

List the three toughest questions you could be asked.

1. _____
   _____

2. _____
   _____

3. _____
   _____

On a separate piece of paper, make a list of the points you want to make in response to each question. Practice your response in your interview role-play.

SECTION K:
OBJECTIONS TO OVERCOME

(Chapter 8, page 55) Anticipate any problem areas you might encounter and plan your strategy to address the objection head on.

Possible problem areas ("I'd like to hire you, but..."):_____

_____

Way to handle this:_____

_____

Possible problem areas ("I'd like to hire you, but..."):_____

_____

Way to handle this:_____

_____

Possible problem areas ("I'd like to hire you, but..."):_____

_____

Way to handle this:_____

_____

Possible problem areas ("I'd like to hire you, but..."):_____

_____

Way to handle this:_____

_____

_____

SECTION L:
SALARY STRATEGIES

(Chapter 9, page 66) What is the current market salary range for this position?

What salary are you going for? _____

What can you deliver in tangible terms that clearly justifies a salary higher than the one you are willing to go for?

_____
_____
_____
_____
_____
_____

A FINAL REMINDER

You are in the center of your own job search and the interview is completely in your control from your point of view.

Your job is to know your value in the work world and to communicate it over and over again until you make the right connection.

We wish you the very best in your search for meaningful and fulfilling employment.

ABOUT THE AUTHORS

TOM JACKSON, chairman of Equinox Corporation and founder of the Career Development Team, Inc., is one of the nation's leading authorities on human resourcefulness, high performance, and the way people deal with their work lives and careers. He is the author of several best-selling books on career development and the job search. More than one hundred thousand people world-wide have participated in his innovative programs.

BILL BUCKINGHAM, president of Equinox Interactive, has over two decades of experience working with dislocated workers and career changers. He has designed and published several innovative and award-winning software programs on career and job search management that have been used by individuals, universities, and corporations throughout North America and Europe.